COMBAT COLOURS

MILITARY AIRCRAFT MARKINGS

COMBAT COLOURS

MILITARY AIRCRAFT MARKINGS

Bob Archer and Peter R Foster

OSPREY
AEROSPACE

Published in 1992 by Osprey Publishing Limited
59 Grosvenor Street, London W1X 9DA

ISBN 1 85532 205 6

Editor Tony Holmes
Page design by Paul Kime
Printed in Hong Kong

Front cover As befits a squadron display aircraft, Phantom FGR.2 XV426 of No 56 Sqn looks absolutely immaculate as it sits on the ramp at its home base of RAF Wattisham. The vicious looking shark's mouth which adorns the detachable nose cone first appeared on a squadron jet (FG.1 XT902) just prior to the 1983 Air Tattoo at Greenham Common. Over the ensuing nine years, several Phantom IIs have worn the customized radome

Back cover Over the years the diminutive Fiat G.91 'Gino' has been the mobile canvas for many budding squadron artists. The Portuguese resprayed an aircraft to resemble a Tiger; the Germans decorated a two-seater with blue and white hoops; and the Italians, who have a natural flair for this type of thing, created this masterpiece. Assigned to 2° *Stormo* at Treviso-San Angelo, this G.91R was chosen to wear this special scheme in celebration of the unit achieving 200,000 flying hours on the type. Recently, 2° *Stormo* replaced its weary 'Ginos' with AMX strike aircraft, this transition also signalling a move to nearby Treviso-Istrani

Title page The Lockheed T-33A, or 'T-Bird' as it is better known, was finally phased out of service within the United States in 1990. This led to a number of other countries retiring their fleets of this ageing aeroplane. Pakistan was one of these operators, and initially withdrew its last surviving dozen aeroplanes. However, after reconsidering its position over suitable airframes to maintain its tasking, half of those remaining T-33As were returned to service, with the remainder being cannibalized for suitable spares. This led to a unique situation due to the country's constitution on the number of units allowable within the Air Force as there was no squadron number plate available to operate the aircraft. Therefore, No 2 Sqn, which had once operated both the T-33 and B-57 and had recently re-equipped with the F-7P, was given a dual tasking and twin flights to operate two vastly differing types of aeroplane. Here displaying very distinctive nose markings is one of the few T-Birds still flying with the PAF today

For a catalogue of all books published by Osprey Aerospace please write to:

**The Marketing Department,
Octopus Illustrated Books, 1st Floor, Michelin House,
81 Fulham Road, London SW3 6RB**

In contrast to the two major powers of the world, the Royal New Zealand Air Force is a relatively junior service, and as such only reached its 50th Anniversary in 1987. To celebrate that milestone a number of aircraft received celebratory colour schemes, with one of the more attractive being applied to this twin-seat TA-4K Skyhawk (NZ6256) belonging to No 75 Squadron at Ohakea Air Base

Introduction

The concept of *Combat Colours* arose some years ago as an exercise to gather, in one volume, all of the special schemes that were being devised to commemorate anniversaries and the such like, especially those not given too much publicity. As the idea grew, so unfortunately did the amount of schemes that were appearing which, to some degree, gave the project an open ended finish and as such, delayed its final production.

As the volume of material began to grow so did the catchment area in as far as what was considered to be a special scheme. In the end, after much discussion, it was decided that in the interests of fairness on those units restricted as to the lengths they could be allowed to go in altering their standard schemes, that anything and everything non-standard would be considered.

This, therefore, gave us licence to include the special one-off schemes for the anniversaries as originally conceived; special display colour schemes which were to be regularly seen on the airshow circuit; strange markings and colour schemes adopted as either one-off trials or applied for specific exercises, and finally some of the more elaborate art work that was appearing in ever increasing abundance.

Having set the criteria, the then near impossible task of deciding what to leave out arose and the finished product is in no way indicative of a lack of effort or imagination of those units not included. Equally the type of shots included are hopefully designed to give the reader a good overall look at these schemes without making the subject static. Having said this however, many striking shots were omitted so as to avoid losing a more overall balance.

Obviously having decided on the whole world as being our catchment area, it would have not been completely practical for the material to have been taken solely by the authors. Therefore our thanks must go out to our friends and correspondents who have contributed towards this book with particular mention being made to Robbie Shaw, Lindsay Peacock, Toshiki Kudu, Dick London, Regent Dansereau, Hubert Barnich, Alec Moulton, Brian Rogers, Wally van Winkle, Paul Bigelow, Paul Bennett, John Dunnell, Harry Gann (McDonnell Douglas Corp), Giacomo Manzon, Gerd van Roye, the late Doug Remmington, Peter Rolt, Sergio Bottaro and M. Ogawa, without whom the final product would not have been possible.

Thanks must also go to those many individuals who devoted their time and energies to producing the schemes in the first place, and to the good offices of the respective air forces for allowing access to photograph them. Hopefully in time a second volume will appear to include much of that left out, and that yet to be conceived

Bob Archer and Peter Foster, England 1991

Right Squadron Commanders' aircraft are often the mounts chosen to be repainted to commemorate anniversaries, this Jaguar GR.1A being prepared for No 54 Sqn's 75th on 16 May 1991 belonging to Wg Cmdr T Hewlett for example. The three Jaguar squadrons based at RAF Coltishall, Norfolk, all celebrated being active for three quarters of a century during 1990 and 1991, with No 54 Sqn choosing to incorporate the blue and yellow chequered design on the underwing tank. A host of squadrons reached their 75th anniversary during 1991, having been formed by the Royal Flying Corps in 1916

Contents

Stars and Bars

Special colour schemes have not been restricted to fast jets as the mighty B-52 Stratofortress (for more than three decades the backbone of Strategic Air Command) has also had additional markings applied for bombing competitions. This example, a B-52H assigned to the 410th Bombardment Wing at K I Sawyer AFB, Michigan, was given invasion stripes beneath the wings and rear fuselage and a World War Two fuselage code '5D-P' to participate in *Giant Strike XI* at RAF Marham in 1981. Whereas the US name for the competition was an indication of the purpose of the meet, the RAF dubbed the event *Double Top* implying the competitive spirit during after hours activities!

Above USAF policy, and particularly that of TAC and USAFE in th eighties, allowed a limited amount of wing heritage to be painted on one aircraft within each unit. Many chose to display markings associated with aircraft or actions of the past. Others, like this 18th TFS 343rd TFW A-10A, chose to honour the township in which the base was located. As such, this rather attractive scheme on the engine nacelle of 81-0993/AK shows Fairbanks as the star of Alaska, even though its home base at Eielson is some 25 miles distant

Left The Fairchild A-10A Thunderbolt II has never been an attractive aeroplane. In fact, serious doubts over its battlefield survivability had been expressed within the USAF, especially when operating in a high threat environment. However, successes in the Gulf during 1991 proved that it was perhaps one of the more capable pieces of equipment used by the coalition forces, and one that can wreak havoc when operating in a relatively threat free environment. One of the units who inflicted such damage on Saddam Hussein's forces was the 23rd TFW from England AFB, Louisiana. No strangers to operating in foreign skies, the Wing's aircraft all sport the distinctive shark's mouth insignia inherited from their days of operating with Chiang Kai-shek's forces in China against the Japanese onslaught in the early 1940s. This particular jet, 82-0665, also displays distinctive artwork inside the ladder housing door, indicating that it was the last A-10A to be delivered to the 23rd 'Tigers' and, in fact, the final A-10A built by Fairchild

The 'European One' green and slate grey scheme was finally adopted in 1978 after a period of trials with more elaborate colour schemes. Initially the A-10As appeared off the Fairchild production line in a two tone grey colour. However, before the awful dark green/grey scheme was adopted as standard, many other patterns including this one known as 'Jaws' were tested. This evaluation was carried out by the 57th FWW at Nellis AFB, and included operational trials within the theatres that the jets would be assigned. Tactically, the final outcome was correct, although the scheme displayed here on 75-0258/WA would have been very useful in early 1991

Impressive line up of eight Fighting Falcons at Nellis AFB, Nevada, painted slate grey and dark green to evaluate the close air support/battlefield air interdiction role as a possible successor to the A-10A Thunderbolt II. The nearest aircraft is YF-16B 75-0752, the second two-seater produced, which has spent most of its career on test work with the manufacturer. The remaining seven are F-16Cs assigned to the resident 422nd Test and Evaluation Squadron, which is part of the 57th Fighter Weapons Wing. The 138th TFS at Syracuse, New York, was the first F-16 unit to convert to the new role, with its aircraft being amongst those deployed to Saudi Arabia for operation *Desert Storm*

Above Stylised marking on the fuselage underside of this 8th TFW F-16A see the competition title imaginatively presented in the shape of a handgun with smoke from the barrel. The wolf's head is the Wing's famous emblem which originated during the war in Vietnam when the unit performed both air-to-air 16 and air-to-ground missions

Right Nellis AFB, which is located to the north east of the gambling mecca of Las Vegas, controls more than three million acres of ranges across the desert wastelands to the north of the base. This inhospitable landscape is covered by ideal airspace where exercises can be conducted without creating a noise nuisance. One such exercise is *Gunsmoke*, which is staged bi-annually to evaluate air-to-ground skills with teams drawn from the tactical fighter community in Europe and the Pacific, as well as the USA. Participating units have applied attractive markings to their aircraft, including these F-16As from the 8th TFW 'Wolfpack', based at Kunsan, Republic of Korea, which took part in the 1985 meet

Above The F-106 Delta Dart is no longer in operational service, although a number are being converted into drone targets. One of the last duties performed by the faithful 'Dart was that of chase plane for the B-1B test programme at Palmdale, California, five aircraft being assigned, including this F-106B which was tasked with the role after spending many years of service with the San Antonio Air Logistics Center at Kelly AFB, Texas. The red tail, with black B-1 silhouette, was replaced by a far more elaborate marking shortly afterwards. The aircraft is seen at Otis ANGB, Massachusetts, wearing an underwing tank from the resident 101st FIS, whose facility is close to Cape Cod

Left Refined tail markings on the same aircraft with the predominant red being reduced considerably by the stylish B-1B, flying in formation with the F-106. The white exhaust emissions from the four-engined bomber and the single-engined fighter are cleverly fashioned from the word CHASE. The five aircraft were withdrawn from service during 1990 at the completion of their pursuit duties, effectively ending the operational career of the 'Century Series' fighters within the USAF

Above A pair of Michigan Air National Guard F-4C Phantom IIs bask in the sun on the visitors ramp at Tyndall AFB, Florida, on a warm October afternoon during exercise *William Tell '82.* Most of the unit's F-4Cs had individual names and appropriate nose art, with 63-7618 being nicknamed 'Double Trouble'. Many of the inscriptions were patriotic, all were colourful and sadly none remain on the unit's current equipment. The 171st FIS, nicknamed 'Six Pack', converted to the F-4C after operating the F-106 for many years, both types featuring the familiar black and yellow cheque scheme. However, the advent of tactical schemes resulted in various shades of grey replacing the colourful markings by the time the squadron had received the F-4D. Like most other 'Guard F-4 operators, the 171st has since received the F-16

Left Another Michigan F-4C, this time 63-7514 inscribed 'Shadow Demon', is seen overflying home territory with the tail hook extended for the benefit of the photographer. The retention of the tail hook was a legacy of the aircraft's naval lineage. When the Air Force decided to order the F-4, the hook was retained as a safety feature enabling the aircraft to be brought to a rapid halt using the arrestor cables fitted at the threshold of most base runways in the event of failure of the aircraft's brakes

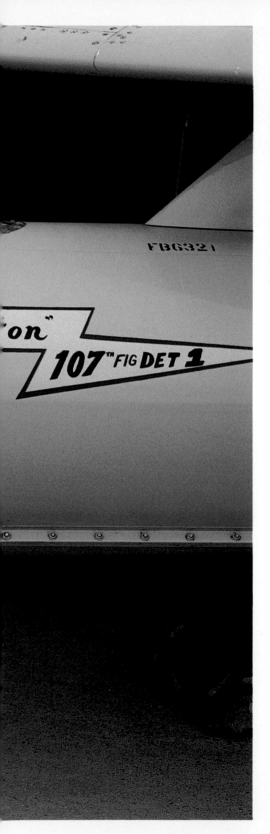

FB6321

"on"

107ᵀᴴ FIG DET 1

Coonass Militia

AF 63 631

Above Unlike most Air National Guard units, which proudly carry the state name somewhere on the tail of their aircraft, this F-4C has only the inscription 'Coonass Militia' which dates back many years as the nickname of the 122nd TFS, Louisiana ANG, based at NAS New Orleans. The unusual two-tone grey camouflage was applied during 1983 and was evaluated by the squadron during a Red Flag exercise at Nellis AFB

Left Air National Guard interceptor units maintain alert status at both their home facility and at a detachment on a frontline Air Force base in another state. The 136th FIS operates from Niagara Falls International Airport, as well as maintaining a full-time detachment at Charleston AFB, South Carolina, some 900 miles to the south. Aircraft are rotated to the Det every two weeks and do not normally carry specific markings for their additional operating location, although F-4C 64-0860 was suitably inscribed NY ANG as 'The Spirit of North Charleston' 107th FIG Det 1, during 1986. The marking was displayed on an underwing tank, along with the customary Spook motif which has for so long been associated with the Phantom II

Left The Air National Guard, although being mobilised to SAC, TAC or MAC during times of conflict, have always enjoyed a certain amount of freedom when it comes to individuality. Therefore, although adopting the normal TAC markings, this 165th TRS RF-4C was allowed a little more licence when attending the *Best Focus '82* competition at Karup in Denmark than its frontline counterparts. In fact, the attractive 'Stars and Stripes' rudder with the 'Eagle' emblem was to be retained for some time to come, although the actual *Best Focus* marking on the nose was only short lived

Above During the late sixties and early seventies the Phantom II was one of the mainstays of NATO, serving in large numbers with more than two dozen US Air Force squadrons in Europe. In this photo a 10th Tactical Reconnaissance Wing RF-4C (the CO's aircraft) lands at RAF Mildenhall shortly before the unit converted to the A-10A Thunderbolt II

Right The state of South Dakota celebrated its centenary during 1989 by repainting the A-7D 70-0996 of the 175th TFS in special anniversary colours. The respray was undertaken by the unit's maintenance shop at their home base at Joe Foss Field in Sioux Falls. During the Corsair's career the aircraft have been operated in a variety of camouflage patterns beginning with the green and tan 'Vietnam' scheme, before being replaced by the ultra low visibility dark green and slate grey 'European One'. Finally the current two-tone grey camouflage was adopted, although none were as eyecatching as this centenary special

Above Frontline and reservist fighter units usually have one aircraft displaying the squadron, group or wing identity on the tail for their commander. Where possible, the serial number of the aircraft is incorporated into the unit designation, this practice being particularly common with the Air National Guard, as in this case where A-7D Corsair II 72-0180 has been appropriately marked for the 180th Tactical Fighter Group, based at Toledo Express Airport, Ohio

Right Although predominantly the domain of fast jets, colourful markings have occasionally been applied to transport aircraft. C-130B 59-5957, which was ordered as a replacement for a USAF example delivered to the Indonesian Air Force while on the production line, was given this attractive tail marking to commemorate the centenary of the state of Wyoming in 1990. The state's heritage is steeped in the tradition of the cowboy, and quite naturally a bucking bronco and rider appears on the centre of the tail. The snow-capped peaks on the fin tip are representative of the harsh weather conditions which prevail throughout the winter

Above Until the eighties the US Navy had always allowed its squadrons plenty of licence when it came to unit markings. This had a plus effect in maintaining a high morale factor, but on the negative side many hours were spent keeping the schemes in good condition, especially when deployed at sea. No stranger to maintaining high profile markings were the squadrons assigned to USS *Midway*'s Carrier Air Wing Five, based at NAS Atsugi, Japan. The A-7As assigned to the wing were quick to adopt both tasteful and attractive markings which included the addition of a shark's mouth around the gaping intake of the VA-93 'Ravens' Corsair IIs. This marking was not only attractive but equally effective in reminding personnel on a crowded flight deck of the dangers associated with getting too close when the engines were being run-up

In contrast to the sixties and seventies, the eighties brought a complete reversal in thinking on the part of the US Navy as regards aircraft colour schemes. This appraisal was to take into account the effectiveness of camouflage as well as the ability of crews at sea to keep the aircraft looking smart in a corrosion infested environment. This led to a complete withdrawal fom high visibility schemes, but produced a number of trials that included this scheme being displayed on the VFMA-321 F-4S. However, as can be seen from the luggage pod, the squadron refused to completely let go of their individuality

The eventual adoption of a flat grey base colour was perhaps inevitable as no scheme blends better with the background. The Marines were one of the forerunners in such dowdiness and applied low visibility schemes with enthusiasm. However, VMFP-3 when detached to MCAS Iwakuni in Japan sought to improve matters by adding a much appreciated shark's mouth, even though still in low-vis colouring. With the end of the venerable Phantom II only a matter of months away such liberalisation was allowed to manifest itself, and resulted in the squadron adopting more colourful markings. Sadly these did not entirely match the schemes of their former glory days, but at least restored the morale factor

Above One of the most flamboyant designs ever to grace the skies was this F-4J of VX-4, whose nickname of the 'Evaluators' adequately encapsulates the squadron's role of weapons compatibility for new and existing fleet aircraft. The squadron is located at NAS Point Mugu, California, and works closely with other units at the station including the Pacific Missile Test Center (PMTC). VX-4 has applied a variety of colour schemes to its Phantom IIs, so it was only to be expected their Bicentennial design would be controversial. The finished result must have taken much thought and imagination and is based on the theme of the star spangled banner and the American Eagle. The result was unique, to say the least

Right In complete contrast to the thinking that was shortly to follow, the 1976 Bicentennial brought about some of the most inspired schemes to be adopted by combat aircraft. VX-4, being a non-fleet unit and therefore less likely to be involved in operational commitments, were perhaps allowed more licence than most. Here F-4J BnNo 153088 is seen in what was perhaps the most outlandish scheme of the period

As a test and evaluation squadron, VX-4 operated aircraft in a great variety of colours, which included several variations of blue, and this very distinctive all black jet. Although the original black Phantom II (BuNo 153783) was to eventually become ZE352 with the RAF, the tradition of an all-black jet displaying the white playboy bunny on the tail was to remain. Here, F-4S BuNo 155539 sports the scheme in 1983, having been on VX-4 strength since being re-assigned from VF-33 'Starfighters' in 1980

VX-4 at NAS Point Mugu operated a number of different F-4s with the Playboy Bunny emblem on the tail during the seventies and eighties, one of which was all white, while the remainder were gloss black. Each of the 'Vandy One' F-4s was assigned to the squadron boss at the time, and with the withdrawal of the Phantom II from service the fin of the last 'Bunny' aircraft was preserved in the Officers' Club at Point Mugu. However, the tradition of a black aircraft was maintained with an F-14A receiving the alluring colour scheme during 1990

Above Another Tomcat and another individual colour scheme, although this one is a fleet aircraft which breaks the rule of low visibility for all carrier assigned squadrons. VF-111, who are better known as the 'Sundowners', have painted double nuts '00' with the sunburst occupying the entire tail for many years, and obviously tradition has triumphed to a degree in this case. This shot was taken on approach to the squadron's home station of NAS Miramar, California, which is the shore base for all Pacific fleet fighter units when not embarked on a WestPac cruise

Right The F-86 Sabre was withdrawn from USAF service during the sixties, with most aircraft being scrapped, although a small number were reprieved from the smelting pot by becoming museum exhibits or being exported. In addition, several hundred were supplied to overseas customers in kit form for local assembly, including the F-86F by Mitsubishi in Japan for the Air Self-Defense Force. With US stocks exhausted, the US Navy acquired more than one hundred of these Japanese F-86Fs during the 1980s to be expended as unmanned targets with the Pacific Missile Test Center. Conversion to QF-86F drone standard was carried out by the Sperry Corporation at their Inyokern facility, with the star and bar replacing the Japanese rising sun. A handful of the F-86s had flown with the 'Blue Impulse' display team and retained their distinctive livery, including this one at NAS Point Mugu, California in November 1990

Left To celebrate the 75th Anniversary of US Naval Aviation in 1986 a number of special schemes were devised. Here TA-4J Skyhawk BuNo 158085 is painted up as the commanding officer's mount of VT-22 'Golden Eagles', based at NAS Kingsville, Texas. The unit normally adopts a tail code of 'B' with a modex in the 200 series fitting in with its sister units of VT-21 and VT-23. However, BuNo 158085, as can be seen, has had the modex altered from its normal 'B-215' to just '275' to commemorate the occasion

Above At NAS Chase Field VT-24 'Bobcats' 75th Anniversary scheme has gone along the lines of navy blue and gold, but has also included a central white stripe to make the finished product even more effective. Still retaining its 'C' tail code, TA-4J BuNo 158723 has received an amended modex to include the figure '75'

Above In celebration of the 75th Anniversary, Training Wing One at NAS Meridian, Mississippi, resprayed this T-2C in an attractive patriotic blue, white and red scheme. Note the small outlined map of the state beneath the star and bar and the position of the Naval Air Station marked in red

Right Another 75th Anniversary scheme for the US Navy is portrayed on this T-2C, BuNo 156721. The Buckeye has served as a basic jet trainer for the US Navy, and as an advanced trainer for several other countries, being developed over the years to its present twin-engined form from the very much underpowered single engined A- and B-versions. The Navy operates the jet trainer with VT-9 and VT-19 at NAS Meridian, VT-23 at Beeville, VT-26 at Chase Field and with the adversary squadrons on both the East and West coasts

Best of British

Right Depicted here over the North Sea is Tornado F.3 ZE907 in the display markings devised by Flt Lt Fred Grundy and his navigator for the 1990 show season. The scheme was, however, to be removed before the year's end as the aircraft was updated for duty with the British forces at Dhahran along with other late model ADV Tornados. This particular aircraft had been delivered from BAe Warton to No 5 Squadron at RAF Coningsby on 25 April 1989, before transfer to No 65 Sqn/No 229 OCU a short time later

Below The RAF has always assigned a specific pilot or pair of aircrew to demonstrate the capabilities of their frontline fighter aircraft during the airshow season at home and on the continent. Amongst the types performing their routine each weekend during 1990 were the Phantom II and the Tornado F.3, the latter crewed by pilot Flt Lt Fred Grundy and navigator Flt Lt Martin Parker. No 229 OCU (Operational Conversion Unit) Tornado F.3 ZE907 was painted in a highly distinctive candy stripe scheme with the Battle of Britain 50th Anniversary emblem on the nose. The Tornado is seen prior to displaying at its home base of RAF Coningsby in June 1990 with the No 228 OCU Phantom FGR.2 display aircraft of Flt Lt Steve Howard and Flt Lt Nige Marks in the background, alongside a pair of Dutch F-16As also painted with air display markings

Amongst the many RAF squadrons who celebrated their 75th Anniversary during 1990 were six operating the Tornado GR.1 with RAF Germany. Each of these six squadrons painted an aircraft in special markings although some were more attractive than others, with this example from No 31 Sqn at Bruggen being one of the most colourful. The preparation of RAFG Tornados for transfer to the Middle East as part of Operation Granby during the autumn of 1990 saw some of the anniversary colour schemes hurriedly replaced by a sand camouflage more suitable for the desert conditions

After serving with RAF Germany since 1970 the Phanton II was finally withdrawn during 1991. Four squadrons were dedicated to ground attack and reconnaissance until replaced by the Jaguar, while a further two air defence squadrons were equipped with the FGR.2 beginning in 1976 to replace the Lightning F.2A. These latter two, Nos 19 and 92 Sqns, moved from Gutersloh to Wildenrath during the first part of 1977. However, the unification of East and West Germany and the elimination of the Warsaw Pact obviated the need to have two squadrons devoted to air defence located close to the Dutch border. No 19 Sqn celebrated its 75th anniversary in September 1990, although the event was delayed two months as crews were at Akrotiri, Cyprus, for *Operation Granby*. No 92 Sqn was not so lucky as the unit stood down in July 1991, 14 months short of its 75th. Undeterred, the unit painted FGR.2 XV408 in an all-blue scheme to match that of its sister squadron, who prepared a similar coloured aircraft, XT899, the previous year

Above Night shot of a No 74 Sqn F-4J (UK) at RAF Wattisham two months before the unit exchanged the former US Navy version for the FGR.2. A thunderstorm rolled across the RAF station as the shot was being taken, with a lightning bolt shattering the black sky above the tail! The black fin apparently stemmed from an F-4J (UK) which suffered mechanical problems on delivery from the USA and was given the extra markings while receiving repairs. The additional fin colours were retained when the aircraft finally arrived at Wattisham and eventually the whole squadron was similarly marked. No 56 Sqn, also stationed at Wattisham, followed, with the commander's aircraft receiving an all-red tail in 1990 which inevitably spread to other aircraft in the squadron during 1991. 56 Sqn should have ceased operating the FGR.2 during the summer of 1992

Left Another view of the No 92 Sqn Phantom FGR.2 wearing its special blue colour scheme at IAT 1991 two weeks after the squadron disbanded

Left The annual Tiger Meet always results in imaginative and attractive designs being applied to participants, with the 1991 event at RAF Fairford bringing together the largest gathering of special schemes. With the United Kingdom hosting the event, No 74 Sqn provided a selection of Phantom FGR.2s for the flying display and the static park, with XV423 exhibiting the nationality emblems of the 14 members. No 74 Sqn is due to operate the Phantom until the end of 1992, thereby becoming the last RAF squadron to fly the type

Above The Phantom FG.1 flew with the Fleet Air Arm (FAA) until 1978 when the aircraft carrier HMS Ark Royal was retired in favour of smaller Invincible class carriers equipped with helicopters and the V/STOL Sea Harrier. Surplus Phantom FG.1s were transferred to the RAF with No 43 and No 111 Sqns both stationed at RAF Leuchars employing the version exclusively. The original plan was for several Navy FG.1 squadrons, although a policy change resulted in No 892 Sqn being the sole operational unit. The revised policy resulted in aircraft intended for the FAA being delivered to the RAF instead, including XV571 which was accepted by No 43 Sqn in June 1969. This aircraft served as the commander's mount with No 43 Sqn until mid-1989 when the unit began to receive the Tornado F.3. XV571 spent a brief period with No 111 Sqn, but unlike many of its companions, escaped being scrapped, instead being placed in storage at Leuchars

The adoption of high visibility markings has gradually crept in as the threat in Europe has receded. Initially it was the last two Lightning squadrons at RAF Binbrook who produced coloured tail sections. This was followed by trials in Germany to help avoid mid-air collisions following the loss of a No 14 Sqn Tornado GR1. RAF display crews saw this as an ideal opportunity to re-introduce distinctive schemes. Here seen at sunset is the 1988 FGR.2 display mount XT900/CO of No 64 Sqn/No 228OCU

Above left No 56 Sqn is scheduled to disband in July 1992 and along with it will go the distinctive red fin and chequerboard Radar Warning Receiver (RWR) of its FGR.2s. This particular aeroplane is seen fully armed with an aggressive shark's mouth painted on the nose. Unlike the Fleet Air Arm FG.1 aircraft, on which the whole nose section was hinged, the radar housing on the FGR.2 was designed to be removed, leaving the AN/AWG-12 radar in-situ. At Wattisham a spare radar nose cone was painted with the shark's mouth for use on display aeroplanes, and as such is not a permanent feature of any one jet

Left Phantom FG.1 XV574 seen high over the North Sea on 6 July 1988. The aircraft was chosen as No 111 Sqn's display aeroplane in August 1985 when it first received its distinctive colour scheme. At that time the yellow on the fin only extended as far as the blade aerial, whilst the black spine was only painted on the upper part, leaving the aircraft serial in black on the air defence barley grey background. By the 1988 season the low-visibility tri-colour had found its way from the base of the fin to the top of the RWR, the yellow extended upwards and the black spine area increased. Although these changes were of a

minor nature the squadron was perhaps unique in maintaining this one-off colour scheme for upwards of five years until the jet was retired in January 1990

Above A sad sight indeed. During a twenty-year career at RAF Leuchars XV574 spent many hours on Quick Reaction Alert (QRA) in one of the two barns adjacent to Runway 09, awaiting the claxton to signify another scramble to investigate an unidentified intruder approaching or violating UK airspace. Many of these were Soviet reconnaissance aircraft probing UK defences, with Leuchars scrambling to meet the lion's share due to the strategic location of the base. XV574 served with No 111 Sqn from 1982 until being flown to RAF Wattisham for storage in January 1990. Surplus Phantom FG.1 models were soon joined by FGR.2s which had reached the end of their planned operational career, enabling eight of the former versions to be reduced to hulks with the removal of engines and other reuseable parts. During the autumn of 1991 XV574 and its seven companions were carted away to a scrap dealer near Newmarket where they were shredded along with more than one hundred surplus Bloodhound missiles!

Above The Jaguar, as a tactical aeroplane in a climate of Cold War tension, has never been one to obtain bright and out of the ordinary markings. However, for the biennial *Bulls Eye* competition held at Husum in 1979 this Jaguar GR.1 (XX732) from No 54 Sqn received this aggressive shark's mouth along with a LeKG.41 zap just beneath the cockpit. This aircraft was one of six deployed to Germany for the competition in October 1979, the others being XX122, XX719, XX722, XX724 and XX727, only one of which is still in front- line service

Right The defence of the northern flank has alway been one of the primary functions of NATO, although Norway and Denmark have been reluctant to have overseas forces stationed permanently on their soil. Therefore, some NATO members have assigned specific squadrons to the defence of this part of Europe, which involves aircraft deploying for exercises. During the winter months much of Norway is covered with snow, requiring RAF aircraft to sport a coat of white camouflage to blend into the terrain during training exercises. Amongst the types which regularly deploy to Norway are Harriers from RAF Wittering and Jaguars from RAF Coltishall. Jaguar GR. 1A XZ355 of No 41 Sqn is seen being prepared for a deployment during early 1990. Twelve months later the aircraft had desert camouflage applied in readiness to stage to the Middle East, although the aircraft remained at Coltishall on standby

Above With many RAF squadrons reaching their 75th birthdays in recent years a spate of anniversary markings have appeared. Unfortunately for some of the earliest squadrons established the opportunities for outlandish markings did not exist. In fact Nos 1, 3 and 5 Sqns produced no significant schemes at all, whilst No 6 Sqn from RAF Coltishall devised this very tasteful modification of its normal markings

Right No 41 Sqn celebrated its 75th birthday during 1991, and produced a very attractive red scheme on one of its aeroplanes. However, the squadron is no stranger to non-standard colour schemes, having adopted the desert pink camouflage for the Gulf conflict. This is, however, a far cry from its NATO assigned region within AF North. The squadron has a primary role of armed reconnaissance in a theatre surrounded not by the plains of Germany, or the desert wastes of the Middle East, but by the mountains of Norway. With an operating base at Bardufoss, the squadron usually deploys to these northern regions at least twice a year. For these exercises one aircraft generally receives an arctic scheme to prove its effectiveness when operating within snowy regions. The camouflage applied prior to the deployment appears to be of a semi-professional standard, whilst the finish applied in-theatre, with temperatures below freezing point, causes the paint to congeal in lumps, as is shown in this shot. This particular aircraft, XZ107, is contrasted against the normal scheme of XZ114 alongside, whilst plugged into a VC10K2 tanker of No 101 Sqn

Above No 2 Sqn, operating from RAF Laarbruch in Germany as part of the 2nd Allied Tactical Air Force, likes to pride itself in being the first fighter squadron of the RAF, beating No 3 Sqn by a short margin. No 1 Sqn starting life as a balloon squadron. To celebrate the first 75 years the squadron devised a scheme in 1988 to depict this achievement, and the aircraft chosen to wear these colours, XZ104, is seen here at low-level over Germany during exercise *Central Enterprise* in June 1988

Above right During 1977 the RAF began trials with schemes considered to be more effective for the scenario they were operating in, with a joint force of Buccaneer units taking on the might of the Americans during one of the first *Red Flag* exercises open to non-US units. In that exercise, as in subsequent ones, the RAF crews more than surprised the US commanders with their ability and professionalism even when operating what were considered by many to be outdated aeroplanes with limited or poor systems. Here seen on approach to RAF Lossiemouth is Buccaneer S.2B XV352, resplendent in a desert scheme and sporting an appropriate red star indicating its role in the packages that it played within the *Red Flag* scenario

Right The Royal Aircraft Establishment has operated a small but varied fleet of aircraft and helicopters for many years often retaining types long after their service career has ended. RAE aircraft are directly operated by the Ministry of Defence Procurement Executive, alleviating the need for low visibility colour schemes as they do not perform operational duties. Many have received a unique red, white and blue 'raspberry ripple' scheme, although a trio of test Buccaneer S. 2Bs were decorated with high visibilty green or yellow areas. The three aircraft were initially stationed at West Freugh, Scotland, for maritime trials

Above Whilst still operating the elderly GR.3, No 3 Sqn went through a period of trials within Germany attempting to find ways of making their aircraft more conspicuous at low-level, and thus reduce the chance of mid-air collisions. All the squadrons in Germany took part in these trials with aircraft adopting various coloured tails. Seen here is Harrier GR.3 XZ130/H in the standard RAF tactical colour scheme, with XV760/K in the background displaying an all-white tail

Right Sharing a role with the No 41 Sqn Jaguars in arctic regions are the Harriers of No 1 Sqn. Akin to the Coltishall Jaguars, the Harriers deploy to their theatre of operations on a regular basis. However, as a rule the aircraft concerned receive a coat of whitewash prior to departure to give them the arctic feel. Here at Wittering is Harrier GR.3 XW919/03 of No 1 Sqn, whilst hovering in the background is a Harrier T.4A of No 233 OCU

No 1 Sqn was the first RAF squadron to convert to the more capable second generation Harrier. Although plagued with problems that have led to the loss of several aeroplanes, the GR.5 has proven itself with its advanced avionics and increased range and weapons load. Seen only as a stop gap before the introduction of the definitive Harrier GR.7, the GR.5s equipping No 1 Sqn continue to play an important part in the NATO defence structure, and have retained their deployment role in Norway. Therefore, as seen here with ZD355/01, the aircraft regularly adopt a white coat for such operations

Masquerading as prototype Canberra VN799, this T.4 version is actually
WT478 of No 231 OCU at RAF Wyton. The aircraft was given this scheme to
represent that worn by VN799 on its first flight 40 years before, and is seen
here taxying out at Wyton on the anniversary of that day with Wg Cmdr
Roland Beamont at the controls – the same pilot who had undertaken the
original flight in 1949. Roland Beamont is one of the most famous British test
pilots having flown for the English Electric Company during the development
of the P.1 Lightning. However, it is as a Hawker Typhoon and Tempest pilot
that Roland Beamont may well be best remembered, and for the fact that he
was shot down over occupied Europe, spending his time in captivity in Eastern
Germany before being forced to walk, with other allied prisoners, out of
Germany away from the advancing armies towards the Russian frontline, from
where he was eventually repatriated

With so many RAF squadrons reaching the age of 75 it may seem quite strange to find one in 1991 celebrating only its 25th Anniversary. No 360 squadron is one of the most junior within the United Kingdom. Born out of a NATO requirement for a dedicated electronic warfare (EW) squadron it formed at RAF Watton in April 1966 and is today funded and crewed jointly by both the RAF and Royal Navy. Celebrating this anniversary gave rise to the adoption of an all-red tail on Canberra T.17 WD955, which is in fact the oldest Canberra still flying. However, when this entered deep maintenance another aircraft in the shape of WJ633 received the same treatment

Above Special markings have become commonplace on aircraft of Strike Command as squadrons reached notable anniversaries or commemorated particular events. Support Command is primarily responsible for flying training, with the majority of their aircraft painted white and red, although a number of No 4 Flying Training Sqn's Hawk T.1s, based at RAF Valley, have received a modified scheme incorporating a blue upper surface and tail. The basic colour scheme was considered sufficiently attractive not to require a new design to commemorate the 70th anniversary of No 4 FTS (which was originally formed at Abu Sueir in Egypt), apart from the appropriate inscription on the nose and fuselage side

Left Now almost totally replaced by the Tucano, the Jet Provost has been the mainstay of flying training for over 25 years. In this period a number of display teams have operated the type, whilst in more recent times this has given way to individual solo routines. The aircraft depicted here, XW374, was one of three painted for the use of the 1987 display pilot Flying Officer Sean Chiddention. Subsequently, Sean has graduated to Jaguar aircraft and was a member of the *Desert Cats* in the Gulf conflict, which is no mean feat for such a young pilot

Above Winner of the Wright Jubilee Trophy in 1985, and subsequently becoming the Jet Provost solo display pilot, Flt Lt Dai Whittingham had two aeroplanes at No 1 FTS painted for the purpose. The aircraft retained the basic Support Command red and white scheme, but adapted it by having the colours run up the tail creating the figure 'One'. This unit will be the last FTS to operate the Jet Provost before converting to the Tucano, whilst Dai Whittingham has since passed onto the venerable Phantom FGR.2. In this shot aircraft XW295 is being flown by Sqn Ldr Erik Mannings

Left No 3 FTS continues to use the Jet Provost T.5A, including this aeroplane, although during 1992 the unit should complete transition to the Tucano T.1

Left Perhaps the most unique Jet Provost in the RAF, and the only ones to be assigned to RAF Strike Command, were the four aircraft operated by No 79 Sqn at RAF Brawdy. The four jets were used by 'C' Flight in the role of training Forward Air Controllers (FAC) to work with air elements, giving them a pilot's eye view of the target and enabling a greater understanding to be reached in the art of FAC. The Jet Provost was becoming expensive to operate and the role was passed onto the Hawk T.1A aircraft, allowing the four jets to retire gracefully. To mark the occasion the two pilots of 'C' Flight decided to jazz up the scheme a little, which resulted in the re-introduction of the yellow training bands as well as a few other pieces not readily identifiable on this photograph, taken on the last day of operations in March 1989

Above Amongst the many RAF units honouring their 75th birthday during 1990 was No 18 Sqn, based at RAF Gutersloh in Germany flying the Chinook HC.1. The squadron emblem of a rampant Pegasus was incorporated into the red and black design applied to ZD980. Gutersloh is the home station of the helicopter assets of RAF Germany, as well as two squadrons of Harrier GR.5/7. However, the planned closure of Gutersloh beginning in 1992 will see the residents move to RAF Laarbruch, which is close to the border with The Netherlands

NATO Allies

Left Commemorative markings have not been restricted to the United States and United Kingdom as several continental air arms have not missed the opportunity to enhance paint schemes. Amongst the special markings applied to Italian aircraft have been those to denote an achievement in operational flight hours. One such milestone was that of 8° *Stormo*, based at Cervia on the east coast of Italy, who completed 50,000 hours with the Aeritalia (Fiat) G.91Y during the mid-1980s. The unit began converting from the F-84F to the G.91Y in May 1970, with both 8° and 32° Stormos at Brindisi being the only two operators of this version. 8° *Stormo* still operates the G.91Y and has since amassed more than 65,000 flight hours. The line up of four aircraft is seen during a goodwill visit to RAF Coltishall in 1988

Below The F-104 Starfighter has been repainted in all manner of attractive and bizarre colours as the long, thin tube shape of the aircraft readily lends itself to fancy paintwork. One of the 'quieter' colour schemes to emerge during the eighties was that of 37° *Stormo*, based at Trapani/Birgi Air Base located at the western edge of Sicily. Although the unit celebrated their 50th anniversary in 1989, the *Stormo* was inactive until October 1984, when it replaced 18° *Gruppo* at Birgi with the F-104S

The Italian Air Force received 24 TF-104Gs which were assembled by Fiat beginning in 1965 for the training role at Grosseto with 20° *Gruppo*. The base was also home for 4° *Stormo* with the F-104S at the time so it was quite natural that the *Gruppo* should merge during mid-1985 under the banner of the former unit as the requirement for Starfighter pilots decreased. During the 26 years that elapsed between 1965 and 1991 the TF-104G accumulated 75,000 flight hours with a remarkably low loss rate compared with the large number of single seat Starfighters which crashed during the same period. The inscription 'Unus Sed Leo' was the motto of 20° *Gruppo,* while the yellow and blue colour scheme and the ferocious lion design were obtained from the unit's badge. The 20 on the nose and wingtip tank were applied to denote the lineage of 20° *Gruppo* with the two-seat F-104

51° *Stormo* at Treviso/Istrana Air Base in north-eastern Italy prepared this highly original design on F-104S MM6869 during 1989 to celebrate the 50th anniversary of the unit. The outstretched black and white cat chasing three mice evolved from the unit emblem, although the design was only applied to the port side, with the aircraft returning to its conventional camouflage shortly afterwards. The F-104S was developed jointly by Aeritalia and Lockheed following a requirement by the Italian Air Force for a successor to the earlier version of the Starfighter, with improvements to the performance. The first production aircraft was delivered to 51° *Stormo* in June 1969. The type is expected to remain in service for most of this decade in its latest F-104S/ASA form which has been designed with enhanced operational and weapons capabilities

The F-104G was the first version of the Starfighter to enter service with the Italians, joining 4° *Stormo* at Grosseto in June 1963, with 3° and 6° *Stormo* converting to the type subsequently. 4° *Stormo* upgraded to the F-104S in July 1970, while 6° *Stormo* converted to the Tornado in 1983, leaving just 3° *Stormo* equipped with the F-104G, although the AMX had started to replace the faithful Starfighter by 1991. Those remaining are flown in the reconnaissance role equipped with the Orpheus pod fitted beneath the fuselage. F-104G MM6579 was painted in this elaborate scheme and unveiled at Verona/Villafranca in November 1989 with just six flight hours remaining, the aircraft being withdrawn from service one month later. It was subsequently placed in storage pending display at Villafranca. The 28 on the engine intake relates to one of the two numbered *Gruppo* which are assigned to 3° *Stormo*

4° *Stormo* at Grosseto had F-104G MM6546 repainted in an overall scarlet red scheme in honour of a reunion of personnel from the car company Ferrari, which took place at the base during September 1989. The Starfighter was finished in the same red colours as that applied to the Formula One racing cars which the company produces. The 'Cavallino Rampante', or prancing horse, is the emblem of both Ferrari and 4° *Stormo*. Some Air Force officials liken the Starfighter to the Formula One car as both are sleek, fast and temperamental beasts that require much delicate handling to fully master. However, in skilled hands both are unbeatable!

Prior to the German *Bundesmarine* retiring the final examples of the F-104G in favour of the Tornado, the 'Vikings' display duo were painted in a distinctive colour scheme for their final season in 1986. The two aircraft were operated by *Marinefliegergeschwader* 2 (MFG2) from Eggebeck in northern Germany, and performed before audiences throughout Europe. The F-104G was delivered to the Navy in 1965 and flown for 20 years before the introduction of the Tornado. Most of the Marine Starfighters were constructed by Fiat in Turin and Messerschmitt at Manching, while a further batch of fifty F-104Gs built between 1971 and 1973 by MBB at Manching contained 36 Marine aircraft

Above Another shot of a 'Vikings' F-104G outside a hangar at Schleswig/Jagel, which is the operating base for *Marinefliegergeschwader* 1, the sister unit of MFG2. The Navy retired their aircraft during the mid-eighties with the final two-dozen aircraft being transferred to the Air Force at Erding Air Base near Munich for disposal by *Luftwaffen Versorgungs Regimenten* 1 (LVR-1)

Above While most special anniversary schemes have consisted of bright colours, *Test Group* 11/*Luftwaffen Versorgungs Regimenten* 1 (TGp11/LVR1) at Erding prepared an aircraft in highly polished natural metal finish for their airshow in September 1986. The stylized tail marking consisted of the LVR1 emblem surrounded by a circle containing badges of all the Air Force units which had operated the F-104. This aircraft was retired from service after the show and placed in storage, although its subsequent fate is uncertain

Above left *Jagdbombergeschwader* 34 (*JaboG*34) at Memmingen was the last operational West German Air Force unit to fly the Starfighter, this F-104G being repainted in an attractive blue, white and yellow scheme, to mark the retirement ceremony on 23 October 1987. *JaboG*34 converted to the F-104 from the F-84F in 1964, performing the fighter bomber role with the type until the introduction of the Tornado

Left An earlier *JaboG* 34 F-104G especially painted in the red, yellow and black colours of the German national flag. The serial of the aircraft was modified to 25 + 50 to reflect the 25th anniversary of the unit and the 50th year of operations at Memmingen Air Base at a ceremony held in May 1984. This particular aircraft had the modified serial presented on the port side only while correct identity 24 + 19 was applied to the starboard side. The aircraft had only a few airframe hours remaining before retirement and was transferred to ground instruction duties at Memmingen, retaining the anniversary colour scheme

Left The West German Air Force was created in September 1956, becoming a member of NATO at the same time. Equipment was predominantly of French, Italian and US manufacture and consisted of transport and training types initially, followed by hundreds of fighter/bomber, reconnaissance and interceptor aircraft. Delivery of these combat types did not take place until the end of the decade, with units being activated shortly before their introduction into service. With many units being formed at the end of the fifties, their silver anniversaries occurred during the mid-eighties. One such unit was *Aufklarungsdeschwader* 51 (AkG51), which was established on 17 July 1959 at Erding with the RF-84F, before relocating to Ingoldstadt one year later. The unit re-equipped with the RF-104G in 1963 and moved to Bremgarten in 1969 prior to converting to the RF-4E two years later. To commemorate the 25th anniversary AkG51 held an air show in July 1984, with a specially painted RF-4E on display

Above left With a Bavarian blue chequered tail and the German national colours in a band around the nose, this Luftwaffe IDS Tornado of JaboG 32 serial 44 + 50, received the scheme to celebrate the unit's 30th birthday. Forming at Lechfeld in 1958 with the F-84F Thunderstreak, the unit converted to the F-104G in 1962, operating the Starfighter until the Tornado appeared on the scene 20 years later

Above Forming at Alhorn in 1961 without aircraft, JG 74 absorbed JG 75 and its North American F-86K Sabres later the same year. Thirty years on, having re-equipped with the F-104G Starfighter in 1965, and the F-4F Phantom in 1974, the unit still forms a fundamental part of the German air defence structure. Upon reaching its 25th anniversary during the latter part of 1986, it painted F-4F 37 + 56 in this rather attractive blue scheme to celebrate the event, and may well continue to operate the type up until the next century

Left Following unification of the two Germanys much of the former Soviet hardware used by the East German Air Force will be scrapped. To mark the last days of East Germany, most of the fighter units, realizing their eventual fate, painted one aeroplane in the spirit of unification. At Laage , one of the most modern bases in East Germany and now home to the new JG 75, JBG 77 'Tiger' Squadron gave one of their Sukhoi Su-22M4 fighter/bombers (546) this attractive scheme. Post unification the aircraft was reserialled 2507, but as it has no prospect of flying in Luftwaffe service lacks any national insignia

Above Also taken at Laage post unification, the sister unit to JBG 77, MFG 28, also produced this example of an Su-22M4 in a scheme of red, yellow and blue. This aircraft, although allocated the *Luftwaffe* serial 2544, chooses to retain its former East German number of 799, as well as the MFG 28 unit badge on the tail. Comparing the two shots it will be noted that the Marine example is of a higher mod state, being equipped with chaff/flare dispensers on top of the aft fuselage section. Sadly all these airframes remain in store at Laage but will, in all probability, be broken up due to the German constitution preventing their disposal to other users

Left *Jagdbombergeschwader* 43 (*JaboG* 43) is currently based at Oldenburg flying the Alpha Jet, but has changed designation since having originally activated on 11 November 1959 at Leck Air Base as *Jagdgeschwader* 72 (JG 72) equipped with the Sabre. The unit received the Fiat G.91R and moved to Oldenburg in 1964, becoming *Leichkampfgeschwader* 43 (LeKG 43) in 1966 before changing to its present title when it upgraded to the Alpha Jet in 1981. *JaboG* 43 celebrated their silver anniversary in November 1984 with an Alpha Jet painted blue and white with black, red and yellow tail and upper surfaces

Above *Bulls Eye* 1979 was hosted by *LeKG* 41 at Husum, and as such saw many of its Dornier/Fiat G.91Rs receive a very attractive shark's mouth, which the nose design of the type wore very well. Here a pair of aircraft including 3254 are seen outside one of Husum's many hardened aircraft shelters. The unit has subsequently re-equipped with the Alpha Jet, many of its former mounts, including this example, passing on to the Portuguese Air Force

These highly original markings were applied to G.91T to commemorate the retirement of the type from *Luftwaffe* service in March 1982, following the introduction into service of the Alpha Jet. The G.91 was operated by several units including *Waffenschule* 50 (WS 50) at Furstenfeldbruck for training until the arrival of the Alpha Jet, *JaboG* 49 being activated in its place to better reflect the combat role of the new type. The blue and white G.91T was placed on display at 'Fursty', adjacent to the control tower

The Piaggio P.149D was one of the first types to enter Luftwaffe service, 76 aircraft being supplied beginning in 1957 and a further 190 being licence built by Focke-Wulf. Many were later sold onto the civilian market, with the surviving Air Force examples being located at Furstenfeldbruck with *Waffenschule* 50 (WS 50) However, every aircraft type eventually reaches the end of its operational lifespan, and the P.149D was finally withdrawn in March 1990, this airframe being painted in a special blue and white design to mark the occasion. An 18-aircraft flypast was performed over Furstenfeldbruck base before the remaining 35 P.149s were placed in open store pending sale. Whilst not strictly combat aircraft, the little Piaggios were instrumental in training thousands of fast jet pilots during 33 years of service

The German Army, or *Heeresflieger*, has also had occasion to commemorate specific anniversaries, with this CH-53G being painted for the 30th anniversary of Mendig at Niedermendig Army Base to the east of the Eifel region in June 1987. The aircraft selected for the ceremony was the fifth CH-53 for the *Heeresflieger*, and the first operational example. Following delivery of two CH-53Gs constructed by Sikorsky at Stratford, Connecticut, VFW built the remaining 110 under licence, with fabrication at Bremen and assembly at Speyer

All-white Mirage IIIR of 33 *Escadre de Reconnaisance*, based at Strasbourg-Entzheim with the battleaxe symbol of the first *Escadron* (ER 1/33) on the tail. The aircraft was painted for the airshow at Entzheim in June 1986, which was staged to mark the replacement of the Mirage IIIR by the Mirage F. 1CR. Note the different presentation of the three dates on the rear fuselage. ER 1/33 was originally 33 *Escadrille* during World War I, having formed in 1914, and in keeping with other French Air Force units which have adopted regional names, is known as *Belfort*

EC 4/7 at Istres painted two of its Jaguars, A67/7-NB and A64/7-NE, inscribed RAMEX 80-89, to represent the nine years of commitment to France's Rapid Reaction Force, and the disbanding of the unit which stood down from operations on 31 July 1989. The unit's position in the French rapid reaction force was taken by EC 3/4, which began working up at Luxeuil on the Mirage 2000N prior to receiving the tactical variant of this strike fighter

Of all the French Air Force types the Sepecat Jaguar has had a greater overseas commitment than any other in recent years. Its role in Chad, Djibouti and the Gulf within the coalition forces cannot be overstated. The irony is, however, that following the takeover of Breguet by Dassault no apparent efforts were made to seek overseas sales for the type, which would have been in direct competition against other Dassault products. Yet of the types in use in France today it is the Jaguar which holds the highest battle honours. The squadron role played by the Jaguar has seen squadrons adopt a variety of desert colour schemes, as depicted here on aircraft A84/11-YJ. During the Gulf conflict the aircraft received a modified wraparound scheme, with code letters being removed from the engine intake to beneath the cockpit

Left The Tiger Meet has been staged since 1961 when the 79th TFS at RAF Woodbridge invited the Lightning F.1s of No 74 Sqn and Mystère IVAs of EC12 to a one-day gathering of units whose squadron motif was that of a tiger. By the end of the year eight tiger squadrons had joined the association, with an annual meet held to establish friendship between representatives of their units. The 1968 event at Woodbridge produced the first of many aircraft in an overall tiger paint scheme, a Canadian CF-104 of No 439 Sqn from Lahr, Germany being the star of the show. Subsequently there have been many other interesting colour schemes, with the G.91R of the Portuguese Air Force being one of the most original. This aircraft was prepared by *Esquadra* 301 when they hosted the 1987 event at Montijo

Above Three CF-101 Voodoos were painted in special schemes prior to the retirement of the type from service and to commemorate the 60th anniversary of Canadian military aviation in 1984. Furthest is 'Hawk One' of No 409 Sqn next to 'Lynx' of No 416 Sqn, while 'Alouette Un' of No 425 Sqn is positioned alongside the unique all black EF-101B of No 414 Sqn. The latter aircraft was leased from the US Air Force during the early eighties to conduct electronic countermeasurers duties for frontline squadrons. Not surprisingly the EF-101B was known as the 'Electric Voodoo', and had the distinction, along with another CF-101B, of being the last flying examples of the type. The last flight was performed on 4 April 1987. At the completion of its duties in Canada the EF-101B returned to the USA, with another Canadian Voodoo being preserved at CFB North Bay in the black scheme

Above Following the demise of the ECM fitted Avro CF-100 with No 414 Sqn, the Canadian Forces took on loan from the USAF this EF-101B, and its 'hot pod' system. The aircraft, although on loan, was allocated serial 101067 following on from Canada's own batch of air defence aircraft. At first it operated in the normal USAF scheme with the Canadian national insignia and No 414 Sqn's black/red striped rudder. However, following tradition, it was inevitable the 'Black Knights' would eventually repaint the aeroplane in the famous all-black scheme. Ultimately it became the last Voodoo in Canadian service, finally being returned to the United States for permanent display at Minneapolis, restored to its former identity of 58-0300

Right Close up of the hawk design on the side of the No 409 Sqn CF-101, which was the second aircraft to be painted in this colour scheme. The original Hawk One was prepared in 1977 to celebrate the 25th anniversary of the squadron, but reverted to conventional grey markings shortly afterwards

Above Apart from Tiger colours Canadian CF-104s have also worn decorative schemes associated with particular squadrons. One such Starfighter was that of No 421 Sqn 'Red Indians', whose stylized design was shown at events in 1983 before the type was replaced by the CF-18 Hornet

Above left The use of two languages in Canada is evidenced by the port side view of 'Lark One' from No 425 Sqn, which had 'Alouette Un' on the other side

Left No 439 Sqn CF-104 wearing the full tiger stripe scheme at the 1981 Tiger Meet, staged at Bitburg Air Base, Germany. Apart from painting the aircraft, crews have often applied tiger colours to their helmets, aircraft chocks, access ladders, and tool boxes. Several different Starfighters were repainted in these colours during the type's 21 years of service in Europe. Other nations who have sent tiger striped aircraft have included the Belgians, French, Germans, Portuguese, and the RAF, whose Puma HC.1 was the first helicopter to bear this design

Right The Canadians have been reluctant to exhibit a CF-18 Hornet in yellow/black tiger stripe as the aircraft would require a complete repaint afterwards, which would be unjustifiably expensive. Whereas the Starfighter could be returned to its camouflage pattern without too many man hours being spent in the paint shop, the grey of the Hornet would be difficult to respray. Nevertheless personnel at Sollingen are to be congratulated for designing such a unique and eyecatching tiger stripe aircraft, while retaining the overall air superiority grey. The CF-18 was one of the representatives at the 1991 Tiger Meet staged at RAF Fairford as part of the International Air Tattoo

Above Most special colour schemes appear to be applied to fast jets or aircraft which are combat capable, with very few elderly piston engined types included. However, the Canadians painted this CP-121 in 1987 when VS/MR-880, alias Maritime Squadron 880 based at CFB Summerside on Prince Edward Island, celebrated the 30th anniversary of the Tracker. The subdued nationality roundel on the rear fuselage has been used as the zero to good effect, while the CS2F-CP121 are the former and current designations which the Tracker was assigned in Canadian service

Left When the *Koninklijki Luchmacht (Klu)* celebrated its 75th anniversary in 1988 a single example of almost every type in operational service received an anniversary scheme. On the whole, these schemes consisted of a red, white and blue cheatline running the length of the fuselage and up the tail, with 'KLU 75' becoming the central feature on the vertical stabiliser. Such schemes were applied to transport types as well as fighters, as illustrated by this Fokker F27M going through its impressive display routine

Above Still on the 75th anniversary scheme, this No 312 Sqn F-16A (J-864) became the *Klu* Fighting Falcon display mount for the 1988 season. The unit was the sixth to convert to the F-16, the last at Volkel air base and also the ultimate user of the F-104G Starfighter in Dutch service

Above A pair of No 311 Sqn F-16As with special tail markings applied for the squadron's 40th anniversary on 1 May 1991. The Dutch, like their neighbours in Belgium, have regularly prepared aircraft for anniversaries with a variety of attractive designs. These two aircraft are seen in flight near their home base at Volkel

Above Right All *Klu* display mounts have had their schemes designed around Dutch national colours, as with Canadair NF-5A K-3019 seen in 1982. The Dutch operated 105 F-5s within four squadrons, the final aircraft being retired in 1991. Most of the surviving aircraft, however, have since been passed on to other users, with this particular aeroplane being delivered to Turkey on 12 October 1990

Right When the NF-5As were withdrawn from service by the Royal Netherlands Air Force, many found their way to the Greek and Turkish Air Forces. However, during their career they were initially operated in a two-tone green and grey camouflage, before gradually adopting various combinations of grey. Without a recognized demonstration team, the Dutch have elected to promote their Air Force through singleton or duo displays at home and abroad. The NF-5 was one of the types which performed these displays with No 314 Sqn at Eindhoven, operating this specially painted aircraft for the 1984 season

Above When No 313 Sqn at Twenthe phased out the NF-5 in favour of the more capable F-16A in 1988 it painted one of its last examples in a special scheme to mark the type's demise. K-3045, depicted here, displays a message of thanks for the sterling service the type gave over the previous 18 years. The aircraft itself actually served with all Dutch NF-5 squadrons, and now continues to serve Turkey in the same capacity having been delivered to Konya on 15 October 1990

Right During 1989 the Dutch Navy (MLD) under the auspices of No 7 Sqn created a display team at De Kooi known as the 'Windmills' utilizing a pair of Westland SH, 14 Lynx helicopters. No 7 Sqn itself operated a mix of UH. 14A, SH. 14B and SH. 14C Lynx's, which in turn are operated under a flight structure. These are not ships' flights as No 7 Sqn is the training unit. The flights have devised artwork for the noses of their helicopters, some of which are known as 'Haddock Flight VE3', 'Snoopy Flight VE5' and 'Pink Panther Flight VE2' which is depicted here

Left 8 *Smaldeel* (Sqn) Mirage 5BA with blue and white tail and fuselage markings to denote 15 years of operations with the French-built fighter. The aircraft is seen overflying the huge oil terminal complex at Antwerp and appears to blend into the surroundings rather well

Above Mirage 5BA of No 1 Sqn painted in a striking black scheme with the unit's thistle motif on the tail formates with the blue and red Mirage of No 2 Sqn over the River Meuse at Dinant during 1987. No 1 Sqn was based at Bierset while 2 Sqn was operational at Florennes

Left A close up view of the No 2 Sqn Mirage 5BA depicting the distinctive shooting star emblem applied for their 70th anniversary in May 1987. The Belgian Air Force has presented some very attractive designs and has not missed the opportunity to commemorate squadron anniversaries or milestones in the service career of specific types. No 2 Sqn has since exchanged their Mirages for the F-16, with a Fighting Falcon being suitably repainted for the unit's 75th anniversary

Above Apart from the RAF, which has squadrons that have reached their 75th birthdays, most of our European partners are slightly younger. Amongst those that came into being following the 1918 armistice was that of 'Foto Sectie' at Evere. This subsequently became 7 *Verkennings Smaldeel, IV Groep, 1 Regiment* Belgian Army. The current day 42 *Smaldeel* takes its lineage from its reformation date in 1955, operating for two years as 'C' Flight No 2 Sqn/RAF at Wahn. To mark the 70 years of photo recce operations, the squadron created this splendid scheme on Mirage 5BR BR15

Seen landing at Beauvechain on return from a weapons detachment to Solenzara, Corsica, is F-16A FA-18, looking resplendent in the attractive scheme devised to celebrate No 350 *Smaldeel*'s 45th anniversary. The 'flames' along the upper fuselage were at one time a standard marking on the unit's CF-100 and Hunter aircraft, but were carried infrequently on their F-104G Starfighters. The squadron is quite junior within the *Force Aerien,* having started life as the first of two Belgian squadrons within the RAF during World War 2

No 31 Sqn is the Belgian Air Force representative unit in the Tiger Association, and quite naturally an F-16A was painted in appropriate markings for the 1985 meet, which was held at Kleine Brogel Air Base. Only two-thirds of the aircraft was repainted in the tiger scheme by design, rather than the squadron running short of paint. Although membership of the Association is worldwide with squadrons in the USA and Australia, the majority of participants are drawn from Europe. However, the 1991 meet included representatives from Czechoslovakia, with other non-NATO forces expected to join in due course

For the 1991 Tiger Meet No 31 Sqn chose a combination of the conventional black and yellow stripes, the grey pattern which seemed to be in vogue at the time. Apart from the time spent physically applying the paint to the aircraft, much consultation occurs prior to the final design being selected. The application of the Tiger Meet colours to each aircraft is normally carried out shortly before the event, with the airframe emerging from the paintshop for approval by the squadron boss. However, before one drop of paint is applied to an aircraft, a full-colour drawing has to be submitted for approval, with no guarantee that an elaborate design will be sanctioned. Thankfully most see fruition

Left Not all schemes are devised to celebrate anniversaries. Of late there has been a tendency to allocate a specific airframe which has sufficient fatigue index available for it to complete a whole display season without requiring a major overhaul for airshow work, the chosen aircraft receiving an attractive colour scheme. The reasoning for this is two fold; initially all aircraft have individual characteristics, and in the display routine it is better for the display pilot to know his mount intimately. Secondly, in choosing an individual airframe it can be monitored more easily to see how such things as the 'g' factor are affecting components. Belgium has over the last few years adopted this policy with its display Alpha Jet. In this shot, the display routine is in the hands of 11 *Smaldeel*, one of three units operating the type from Brustem

Above This No 7 Wing Alpha Jet from Brustem painted red, yellow and black, wore the number 40 on its tail to commemorate an anniversary during 1987. The anniversary does not appear to be in connection with the Wing, which was formed in December 1950, or the three squadrons, Nos 7, 9 and 11 *Smaldeel*, which were established around the same time. Nevertheless, the colour scheme was a welcome addition to the airshow circuit during that year

Left Alpha Jet AT-29, wearing the colours of the Belgian national flag, has seen several seasons on the display circuit. Although not the most impressive of aeroplanes, the Alpha Jet has successfully performed both the basic and advanced jet trainer roles for the Belgian Air Force. Based at Brustem, the air force operates 32 examples of this docile little jet within the structure of three training squadrons; Nos 7, 9 and 11 *Smaldeel*

Above No 11 *Smaldeel* celebrated their 70th anniversary in 1989, this Alpha Jet receiving an attractive four-tone colour scheme. These colours were selected from the squadron badge consisting of a grey bat with black wings on a yellow triangle. Not surprisingly, the squadron chose AT-11 as the aircraft to receive the anniversary artwork. In keeping with the need for the Belgian Air Force to maintain stringent control on finances, these special colour schemes frequently remain on the aircraft until major overhaul, when they are repainted

Exotica

Left Sweden, by virtue of its policy of neutrality, primarily operates indigenously produced types which has left it in a position of difficulty when it comes to effective dissimilar close air combat training (DACT). To counter the problem of having only two frontline types when involved in DACT, the air force has adopted a policy of painting the aircraft with individual tactical code numbers on the upper surfaces of the wing to aid identification of friend and foe. Seen preparing to take off from the now closed base of Tullinge are a pair of 1st Squadron/16th Wing J35F-1 Drakens, with the tactical codes clearly visible on the wing

Below Today, the sole operator of the J35 Draken in Sweden is F10 Wing, based at Angleholm on the country's west coast. The wing has three squadrons, one of which includes the twin-seat Sk35C aircraft, whilst all of the others have recently re-equipped with the upgraded J35J version of this ageing fighter. The aircraft depicted here is in fact a J35F-1 which lacks the infrared 'IR' sensor under the nose section. This aircraft (35468) was chosen as the Draken solo display aeroplane for the 1989 and 1990 shows, and received this atttractive red fin with the squadron ghost motif, whilst the tactical code, 66, was moved to the aft tail section

Above The Japanese Air Self-Defense Force (JASDF) operated more than 200 F-104J Starfighters from 1962 until the mid-eighties when they were replaced by the F-4EJ and F-15J. The JASDF had a requirement for manned drones with QF-104J 46-8592 making its first flight shortly before Christmas 1989 at Nagoya/Komaki. Aftr several test flights the drone was airfreighted by C-130H to Iwozima for a 15-month evaluation prior to a further 29 conversions taking place. The aircraft was painted with red tiptanks and tail, and white wings to enhance visibility

Above right Production of the F-4EJ for the JASDF finally ran to some 140 Mitsubishi-built Phantom IIs equipping some six *Hikotai* at five locations. All of these appeared in a standard air defence grey colour scheme, but during the eighties trials were carried out on other schemes to see if the breaking-up of the markings would make the aircraft harder to spot. One such scheme tested was this blue/grey splinter pattern applied to aircraft 47-8335 of No 306 *Hikotai*, based at Komatsu

Right F-4EJ of No 306 *Hikotai* based at Komatsu Air Base with special decoration for the annual gunnery competiton. Competitors have painted their aircraft in a variety of camouflage and high visibility colour schemes, with some aircraft displaying ferocious sharks' mouths. The stencilling on the dark areas is readily apparent, as are the two US style 'MiG kills' which were probably applied in recognition of an intercept rather than the physical destruction of an 'enemy' fighter

Above Apart from the trial schemes that were applied during the early to mid-eighties, at the annual air combat and gunnery competitions units applied their own special marks to those aircraft participating. This in turn led to some very attractive schemes emerging such as this No 306 *Hikotai* aircraft seen taxying out at Hyakuri during the 1986 event. The scheme is in fact only water soluble paint applied over the standard grey, and was easily removed following the competition

Right F-4EJ 37-8319 of No 303 *Hikotai* seen in 1986 wears not only the Green Dragon motif depicting the guardian god of the sacred mountain HAKUSAN close to its base of Komatsu, but also an additional winged dragon emblem on the splitter vane. Since this photo was taken the squadron has converted on to the McDonnell Douglas F-15J Eagle, becoming the first Phantom II unit to do so

Left Another country conscious of the problems associated with DACT is Japan. To counter this No 304 *Hikotai* at Tsuiki gave some of its aircraft blue fuselage stripes to make visual identification easier, and hopefully reduce the possibilities of a mid-air collision whilst practising tactics to counter the close air threat. It also enabled two v two missions to be flown more easily

Above Now that many of the problems affecting South Africa are being resolved the armed forces have been able to stand down from their high state of alert. In doing so, radical defence cuts have seen the demise of several types including the withdrawal of the last Dassault Mirage IIICZ fighters. Although many of these early Dassault jets have been completely rebuilt by Atlas and converted into the advanced Cheetah fighter, this particular aircraft, serial 800, was the first of the original batch of 18 jets purchased from France. It is seen here at Hoedspruit in October 1990 at the 50th anniversary of No 2 Sqn, where it received this very attractive black scheme. Today, however, no Mirage IIICZs are left flying within the SAAF, the last one being withdrawn shortly after this photograph was taken

The Pakistani Air Force opened this book and to some degree it is fitting that it should close it also. No 2 (Composite) Sqn at PAF Base Masroor operates a mix of types in completely differing roles. Not so long ago the squadron operated the Martin B-57 Canberra alongside the venerable T-33A in the target facilities role. However, akin to the 'T-bird' problems of maintaining a type no longer in service elsewhere, whilst an arms embargo remains in existence with the one possible supply source led to the B-57 being withdrawn from service in the mid-eighties. However, having said this, many of the aircraft are still held in operational reserve, including this very well maintained B-57C (53-3846), with its nose art of 'Baba'